Interiors

MARTYN THOMPSON

DESIGNED BY KIRSTEN WILLEY

FOREWORD BY ILSE CRAWFORD

hardie grant books

MELBOURNE · LONDON

before
ding
der.

different border

→ PROPS

round
edges →

↑

Hi Iris, Some colours for the
snail plate. Let me know
your thoughts? I think the
greens look good.
Best Regards

#2

Nieuwe
kleuren
voor de slak.

①②③④⑤

#4

Aga
becau

CONTENTS

FOREWORD

ONE DAY IN THE EARLY nineties at the magazine I was editing at the time, I came across some pictures taken by a young Australian fashion photographer of his own flat in London. There was something about them I was really taken with, something very different to the picture perfect interiors photography that was typical of the time. They were dark, cinematic almost, and focused on the atmosphere and feeling of the space, and the sense of inhabitation. Then I met Martyn Thompson ... a very different animal to many of his photographic peers. For one thing, he didn't dress head-to-toe in designer black. For another, he was genuinely interested by what was in front of the camera and in capturing that, rather than seeing what he was photographing as something to arrange in his own image. Being untrained in photography as such, he had his own very different perspective. Martyn had come to photography by accident when shooting textiles he had designed, and found he was better at the photography than the textiles. And maybe because of that lack of official education he has never stopped looking and learning. Last time we worked together he had a new baby — a large plate camera, all the better for the long exposures that have a special quality. His particular gift is a mastery of light, which he seems to be able to capture even where there is none. His pictures are illuminated in a manner that gives life to the interiors he shows – almost painterly.

The places in this book are alive and complex, messy and marvellous. But always perfectly framed, from the poise of Francisco Costa's walls to the teetering piles in his own apartment. Martyn loves to study the visceral process of creativity: he observes the spectacular intensity of Max Gimblett's library as compared with the cool of his studio; Hella Jongerius's combination of fantasy and industry; and Achille Castiglioni's incredible accumulation of inspiration. And he revels in shadows, which gives his pictures a powerful presence, filling the interiors with a poetic beauty — a long way from the dazzling light of a lot of photography today.

We have worked together now for nearly twenty years — on magazines, books, and photographing the studio's interior projects. Much has changed. Martyn moved from London to New York. He has diversified and now also paints and does film. But some things have not. He still nurses an unrequited love for Debbie Harry. He never mixes green and red in his salads. He is extremely funny. He is fascinated by chaos but is himself totally tidy. And he is truly intrigued by the people and places he photographs.

Ilse Crawford
studioilse

Holt Harrison

HOLT HARRISON is where model-turned-property-restorer Liddie Holt-Harrison lives with her husband Howard in England's west country. I got excited the instant I saw it — I just knew I could take great photographs here. Liddie's taste is fantastically macabre. I'd been forewarned about the amount of taxidermy but hadn't been expecting such a haven of demented Victoriana. Growing up in Australia where most things are new left me loving the crumbly quality of ancient buildings, and this one is scattered and crazy, with the eyes of dead animals looking at you from every corner. Liddie had lots of live animals as well — cats and dogs. Two of her dogs even made it into the final photograph.

LESLEY CRAWFORD is a film and TV set designer whose Sydney warehouse conversion, where she lives with partner, Dennis Smith, was once a spare parts factory. When I photograph someone's home I wander around it first, find the bits I like, feel the light, then start looking through the camera to dissect how my photographs are going to come together. It's almost like working through an equation. Lesley's place was abundant in opportunity. Virtually everywhere I looked there was something to shoot, and her taste is eccentric in that uniquely Australian way — her place so full of 50s and 60s kitsch that you almost don't know whether you are in a store, a prop house, or someone's home. It was a real throwback for me, growing up in Sydney in the late 70s when places seemed packed with this kind of paraphernalia.

Lesley Crawford

Vincent Van Duysen

I first met Belgian architect VINCENT VAN DUYSEN in the mid-90s when I was working with Ilse Crawford on our book *Sensual Home*. Vincent's trademark is a very beautiful muted palette and a really sophisticated use of texture, combining the rustic with highly refined elements. This is a very old house and it highlights his ability to be ancient and contemporary at the same time. That's the real skill. Something you feel in Antwerp is a respect for craft and history. His wall treatments are incredible. The paint appears flat but is subtly layered to create real depth. Doing it justice took time and consideration. In fact, what was supposed to be a two-day shoot turned into three, because I was determined to get it just right.

Francisco Costa

FRANCISCO COSTA's apartment overlooks the Empire State Building in New York. I liked it the moment I set foot in it. Like a Savile Row tailor, there is real attention to detail and the workmanship is impeccable. His apartment's style has been likened to his design work for Calvin Klein Collection — his beautiful use of the monochrome palette which streamlines the eclecticism of his furniture collection. This apartment is a clear reflection of the man himself. His personal style and his interior style are totally integrated.

Johansson D'Agostin

JOHANSSON D'AGOSTIN is a favourite shoot of mine. It's all about the mood and the details. The pictures show the studio and home of designers Gunn Johansson and Pierangelo D'Agostin — she's Swedish and he's Italian. Their whole environment appealed to me because there was such a relaxed sense about it. Nothing about this couple was precious. They really trusted me and that comes through in the spirit of the pictures. I love the simplicity — the stripped-back floors and ceiling, which are somehow sparse yet simultaneously rich, and the punctuating use of the colour red.

Evan Snyderman

EVAN SNYDERMAN's Brooklyn place used to be an old school and was awash with retro chic, which is his business. He's a furniture dealer, one of the owners of R 20th Century Design, and when I first moved to New York I was a frequent visitor to the shop in Tribeca. Later I found myself shooting his home. When I first began photographing people's houses I'd basically completely redecorate, take the photographs, and then move everything back again. It was exhausting. This is one of the last times I did any of that, having to rearrange his living area to get that shot of his amazing semi-circular sofa. Why did I stop? Life is a process of letting go. These days, I let places speak for themselves.

John Derian

The JOHN DERIAN assignment was a complete pleasure. *Vanity Fair* wanted a visual portrait of the artist and designer, so it was all about John, his New York home and studio, his house in Cape Cod, and his work – decoupage – which is represented in this first image. Walk into any of his environments and there are umpteen vignettes ready to shoot. His taste is incredible. It's quirky and kooky, neither masculine nor feminine but full of character, humour and beauty. When John first went to the Cape he uncovered wallpaper peeling off the walls and he's left a lot of that. He doesn't try to make something look new: quite the opposite – he lets the cracks and imperfections shine. It's incredibly charming.

Thomas O'Brien

THOMAS O'BRIEN is a furniture and product designer, and the first thing that struck me when I walked into his New York apartment was that I'd never seen so many pictures in my life as there were on his walls. The man is a true collector. He's also renowned for his astonishing work ethic, and that energy is reflected in the sheer volume of objects he has made and his passion for beautiful things. The challenge was keeping that sense of abundance without making the photographs look cluttered. Thomas is also a very handsome man, very good at being photographed in the way that models are. It is wonderful when someone is as comfortable in front of the camera as he was. It makes life so much easier.

Achille Castiglioni

I loved shooting ACHILLE CASTIGLIONI because he just had so much stuff
everywhere — piles and piles of objects in his Milan studio, great rows of stamps
and cardboard boxes. A lot of order in a lot of chaos, which to me is very Italian.
I shot his home and workplace, and the whole thing was a voyage of discovery because
before I got there I had no idea of the breadth of this amazing man's design work. He
was a real character, too, wanting the photographs to have more and more objects in
them when they looked pretty busy already. The portrait happened unexpectedly, after
he suddenly grabbed those amazing glasses. He was 84 and although he didn't seem
that frail to me, he was actually quite unwell. Sadly, he died shortly after this shoot.

Italian jewellery designer ELSA PERETTI is a larger-than-life character both in height — she's Amazonian — and in temperament. I've shot her twice but this first time for Australian *Vogue* was a turning point. She fascinated me with stories of Warhol and Dali and her extraordinary passion for her own art opened my mind to a new world of creative possibility. In fact, this shoot marks the moment when I truly started focusing on interiors and still life. We stayed with her for a week in the Catalan village of Sant Martí Vell — most of which she owns. It's a long time for a single shoot. We ate meals and drank together, as well as planning the shots. We became part of Elsa's life. It was a totally magical experience, and a very unusual one, where we'd only start shooting at 4 o'clock in the afternoon. Why? Let's just say we had some very late nights.

Andrew Egan

Grey is ANDREW EGAN's favourite colour.
His business is named 'cool gray seven', after
the Pantone swatch. Grey appears in his
clothing, in his graphic design work, and even
his bedroom is decked out in a very dark grey
known as 'leadpipe'. This is his New York
apartment, shot for British *Elle Decoration*,
where I wanted to really show his graphic
sensibility. We're very close — he's always been
my biggest fan and supporter. He loves playing
the cello so I had to have this instrument in a
photo because it says something very personal
about him. The shot ended up being almost
entirely black, which technically speaking is not
as hard as it might sound, as light plays onto the
blacks creating shade and shape. I didn't want
to take Andrew's cello out of its case because
I loved the effect of black on black. It is so chic.

Sonja Nuttall

SONJA NUTTALL is an English fashion designer from Liverpool and these pictures are of her old apartment in the East End of London. She has great taste. I love that opening image. There's something about the juxtaposition of that very sleek-looking car — against the concrete, brick and metal. The door is open because an open door is more suggestive than a closed door. It adds anticipation to the image. Someone has just gone in, or come out. Sonja herself has a beautiful energy and that shot of her in the green was actually taken when we were all on vacation in Hawaii. It was just too adorable to not include it.

Fromental

FROMENTAL is the business name of wallpaper designers Tim Butcher and Lizzie Deshayes, and this is their home in Notting Hill, London. Usually before I photograph a place, I'll visit it or at least see scouting pictures. This I came to completely cold — I was in London for just a day or two after my trip to Vincent's house in Antwerp for French *Architectural Digest* and they asked if I could shoot this too. It was easy, though, not just because it was such an intense, rich environment but because I found I really loved what they do. I couldn't live with quite this much chinoiserie in my home but I have always had a very soft spot for it.

Spitalfields

The SPITALFIELDS house is in the east end of London.
It's often rented out as a location and I used to shoot here
a lot, mainly fashion and accessories stories. I grew up
in Sydney, where basically things are new, so when I first
arrived in Paris and London I found this kind of antiquity
incredibly appealing. Floorboards and walls are marked from
hundreds of years of use. You don't have to work at creating
an atmosphere. That said, I can't help but tinker. I found that
teddy bear in the cupboard and put it on the floor, as though
it had just been discarded. I like a picture to be believable —
a sense of the home being lived in — and propping the bear
up facing the camera would not have felt right. What I do is
make believe that things are not staged.

Church Point

CHURCH POINT is a house on Sydney's northern beaches where my friends Lee and Guy Mathews lived. I used to visit every year when I came back to Australia and I've photographed it repeatedly. I always loved this house. It represents an easiness of life — everything is worn, nothing is precious, yet it is all still visually stimulating. It feels like a real working home to me. I met Lee years ago and we designed clothes together back in the 80s. We went to New York in 1984 and did my first reportage shoot — delicatessens of Manhattan for *Vogue Entertaining*, where Lee was art editor. That trip was significant, as it's when I became serious about being a photographer.

Seadrift

SEADRIFT is the much-loved beach house of interior
designer Richard Livingston and his partner Jim Brawders,
in Quogue on Long Island. It was an old barn that has had
a varied life — from a Navy rec hall to an artist's studio.
It's entirely nautically themed, which is not something
I necessarily warm to, but the execution here was spot-on.
I shot it for American *House & Garden*. One side effect
of going into people's homes is that every now and again
I will see something they have and think 'I must do that'. It
happened here with the tongue-and-groove wood panelling,
which I saw, absolutely loved and have since used on my own
kitchen cupboards. It's beautiful, both here and in my home.

Sean Macpherson

SEAN MACPHERSON is a hotelier I met when I photographed his Maritime Hotel in Manhattan. Somehow I'd been expecting his home to be a sleek bachelor pad and not something as liveable and olde-worlde as this. It's very layered as an environment; every part of it has so many different colours, patterns and fabrics. My favourite image is the second one because there's something a little odd about it. The shapes within it are lovely — it's got those great curves and lines — and then you notice that beautiful saddle, which was just sitting there when we arrived. Photographs come so easily when things genuinely surprise you.

DAVE ALHADEF calls his Brooklyn home
a beautiful mess. I agree. He's a friend of
mine and his place is full of contemporary
design and funky things because that's what
he does — sells furniture and artifacts in
his Future Perfect stores. I shot this for
British *Elle Decoration* and really enjoyed
working in the raw loft space. It makes a
perfect setting for Dave's groovy, modern
furniture. It's a very playful environment.
I got a bit fussy when I shot the bed, as I often
do, and spent what felt like hours making it
look as though someone had just gotten out
of it. When in doubt, I add a glass of water.
And then sometimes take it away again.

Highland Lodge

HIGHLAND LODGE is an amazing post-modernist castle hidden away in a remote part of Scotland. The interiors were done by Suzy Hoodless, who suggested I shoot it for American *House & Garden*. The challenge was to convey its extraordinary proportions and the brilliant effect of mixing super-contemporary objects with antique ones. A lot of these pieces are one-offs, suitable for a museum. The outside shoots were fraught because the air was alive with biting midges. We were covered head to foot in netting which I had to whip off every time I took a shot. It was like being in Alfred Hitchcock's film *The Birds*. Even so, I couldn't resist jumping into the loch. That water was the coldest I have ever swum in.

HELLA JONGERIUS really surprised me. She's a Dutch designer I shot in Rotterdam for American *House & Garden*, just after her Milan showing of the animal pots in that final image. She and her team constructed animal hats to reflect the collection – that's Hella in the rabbit ears opposite – and while I love photographing artists and craftspeople because they're so inspiring, they rarely take things as far as Hella did. I knew she was preparing a meal in her studio garden, and that I was going to photograph it. That's not unusual. But very rarely does somebody turn such a thing into a moment of bewildering fantasy.

Hella Jongerius

New Zealand artist MAX GIMBLETT is a very big character who has lived and worked in this Bowery loft in New York since the early 1970s. I loved the overflowing jumble and the way his tools formed still lifes on their own. What struck me most was the directness of his character — formidable. He's best known for creating quatrefoils, and my keenest memory is of shooting him while he was working. He would dip his pen into the ink and make a huge 'humph' sound while creating his shapes. There was something almost primal about it, yet the end result was a beautiful drawing.

KRANZBACH is a very unusual spa in southern Bavaria that Ilse Crawford had me photograph after she finished designing the interiors. Working with Ilse is incredibly easy. She's a Leo and I'm an Aquarian — perfect match or nightmare, according to astrologers. What's magical about our relationship is that it has never required an abundance of discussion. My visuals tend to meet her thoughts very harmoniously. That is my assistant Seth in the pool. Invariably, the photographer's assistant ends up in photographs in one guise or another. A perk of the job — or not, depending how many times I have to do the picture.

kranzbach

ANNA SUI opened the door of her New York city apartment to *W* magazine and, through them, to me. This was my first job for *W* so it was very important that it went well. Luckily, it did. The instant I stepped into Anna's home I felt the magic of it — that rich whimsy and touch of 'Alice in Wonderland' which wafted beyond that beautiful, hand-painted chinoiserie wallpaper into the very heart of her domain. Its magic left its mark on me. In fact, I think this opening image is one of the best interior portraits I have ever taken. The key is the movement in that curtain — it breathes life and intimacy into the shot. Every time I look at this I wonder why I don't use that technique more often.

THANK YOUS

Thank you to Andrew Egan for his endless support of
my work and to Jane Roarty, without whose persistence
I may never have ventured into this world of interiors.
To Ilse Crawford for her beautiful foreword and to
Kirsten Willey who brought this book to life.

To Hardie Grant, and everyone whose house I have
photographed, and the many editors and stylists who have
helped and supported me: Jocelyn Beaudion, David Clark,
Ilse Crawford, Lucy Gilmour, Fiona Golfar, Wendy
Goodman, Mark Jacobson, Marie Kalt, Karen McCartney,
Mallery Roberts Morgan, Michael Reynolds, Mayer Rus,
Amanda Talbot and Pilar Viladas.

To my many co-workers through the ages: Pete, Tim,
Bruce, Tara, Chantal, Hamish, Simone, Nina, Matt, Ryan,
Seth and Trevor, and a special thanks to Evan Strang, who
worked so tirelessly preparing all these images for print.

And finally, thank you to my family for all their
encouragement over the years.

PAGE CREDITS

p007 studioilse.com
p008 holtharrison.co.uk
p034 vincentvanduysen.com
p044 calvinkleincollection.com
p054 unmomentonordico.com
p066 r20thcentury.com
p072 johnderian.com
p084 aerostudios.com
p094 achillecastiglioni.it
p104 tiffany.com
p116 coolgrayseven.com
p122 sonjanuttall.com
p130 fromental.co.uk
p144 leemathews.com.au
p156 seadrift-quogue.com
p168 theboweryhotel.com
p178 thefutureperfect.com
p186 suzyhoodless.com
p200 jongeriuslab.com
p206 maxgimblett.com
p218 kranzbach.de
p234 annasui.com
p240 martynthompsonstudio.com

PUBLISHED in 2011 by
Hardie Grant Books (Australia)
Ground Level, Building One,
658 Church Street,
Richmond, Australia 3181
www.hardiegrant.com.au

Hardie Grant Books (UK)
Second Floor, North Suite,
Dudley House,
Southampton Street,
London WC2E 7HF
www.hardiegrant.co.uk

Publishing Director: Paul McNally
Copy Editor: Helen O'Neill

Colour reproduction by Splitting Image
Printed and bound in China by C & C Printing

Concept, editing and art direction by Kirsten Willey.

National Library of Australia Cataloguing-in-Publication
Data: Thompson, Martyn. Interiors/Martyn Thompson.
ISBN 978 1 74270 234 6 (hbk.)
Interior design. Interior design--Pictorial works. Interior
architecture. Interior architecture--Pictorial works.
Decoration and ornament, Architectural. Decoration and
ornament, Architectural--Pictorial works. 747

hardie grant books
MELBOURNE · LONDON

MARTYN THOMPSON

To say that MARTYN THOMPSON changed the way interiors are photographed over the past 20 years would be an understatement. Into the traditionally stark images of perfectly styled rooms, Martyn has brought light, shade, texture and, most importantly, a sense of lives lived and creativity unleashed. Part of this visual language comes from his background as both a textiles designer and fashion photographer. Another part must be influenced by his global vision and experience; the English-born, Sydney-raised photographer has travelled the world, lived in London and Paris, and now calls New York home. There is an intimacy to his photographs, and indeed many of those included here are of the homes and work spaces of friends and colleagues, making this book a very personal project.

Martyn's portfolio consists of both editorial features in prominent magazines and advertising campaigns for high profile brands. These include Elle Decoration, British Vogue, W, House & Garden and Architectural Digest, with work for Tiffany & Co, Ralph Lauren, Gucci and Hermès. He's co-authored Nikki Tibbles' book, Wild At Heart and photographed both of Ilse Crawford's books, Sensual Home and Home is Where the Heart Is.

DEDICATION
This book is dedicated to friendship and, in my life, the particular friendship of my closest ally — Penny Galwey. She has weathered many a storm with an available ear and an always loving heart ... I love you, PG.

254